american
MUSIC MILESTONES

AMERICAN
POP

HIT MAKERS,
SUPERSTARS,
AND DANCE
REVOLUTIONARIES

ARIE KAPLAN

TFCB
TWENTY-FIRST CENTURY BOOKS
MINNEAPOLIS

NOTE TO READERS: some songs and music videos by artists discussed in this book contain language and images that readers may consider offensive.

Twenty-First Century Books
A division of Lerner Publishing Group, Inc.
241 First Avenue North
Minneapolis, MN 55401 U.S.A.

Website address: www.lernerbooks.com

Library of Congress Cataloging-in-Publication Data

Kaplan, Arie.
    American pop : hit makers, superstars, and dance revolutionaries / by Arie Kaplan.
       pages ;   cm. — (American music milestones)
    Includes bibliographical references and index.
    ISBN 978–0–7613–4504–6 (lib. bdg. : alk. paper)
    1. Popular music—United States—History and criticism—Juvenile literature.
    2. Music—Social aspects—United States—Juvenile literature.   I. Title.
ML3477.K365 2013
781.640973—dc23   2011046501

Manufactured in the United States of America
1 – CG – 7/15/12

CONTENTS

OUT WITH THE Old...

chapter 1

Crooner Bing Crosby was one of the top-selling pop artists of the twentieth century. Listeners loved his smooth baritone voice. His biggest career hit and most widely recognized song is "White Christmas" (1941).

SO WHAT EXACTLY IS POP MUSIC? IS IT THE BEATLES SINGING AN INNOCENT LOVE SONG LIKE "SHE LOVES YOU" (1963)? OR IS IT KATY PERRY SINGING AN EDGY, PROVOCATIVE TUNE LIKE "I KISSED A GIRL" (2008)? ACTUALLY, IT'S BOTH.

The term *pop song* dates back to the early 1920s. But back then, pop tunes weren't necessarily the music of young people. From the start of the twentieth century until the early 1950s, pop music was simply music that was popular with a wide range of listeners. It was wholesome family fare such as Broadway show tunes and big band music. The earliest pop musicians were bandleaders such as Cab Calloway and Benny Goodman or singers such as Frank Sinatra and Ella Fitzgerald. Parents and their children listened to exactly the same type of music.

Eventually, pop music became a type of music that was popular mostly with teens. It could be any type of music—rhythm and blues (R & B), bubblegum, or disco—just as long as young people loved it.

Known as the First Lady of Song, Ella Fitzgerald originally wanted to be a dancer. Her vocal career spanned almost six decades, and she wowed listeners with her vocal range; her improvisational skills; and her pure, effortless sound.

FAMILY-FRIENDLY POP

In the 1920s and the 1930s, many Americans listened to their music on the radio. On weekends, they went to big dance halls such as the Savoy Ballroom in Chicago, Illinois, to dance to the music of their favorite bands. Popular songs in the 1920s included Al Jolson's "California, Here I Come" (1921), Arthur Gibbs's "Charleston" (1923), and Ace Brigode's "Yes, Sir! That's My Baby" (1925). These songs were upbeat and danceable. They had a feel of optimism and fun.

By the 1930s, the Great Depression had hit. Most families in the United States suffered economic hard times. Popular music during these years helped people escape their troubles, even for just a little while. Singers such as Art Tatum, Fred Astaire, and Bing Crosby sang about romance and beauty in songs such as "Cheek to Cheek" (1935), "You Must Have Been a Beautiful Baby" (1938), and "Tea for Two" (1939).

World War II (1939–1945) broke out in the late 1930s. Americans entered the war in 1941, and popular music went to war too. The pop music of this period included songs such as the Andrews Sisters' "Boogie Woogie Bugle Boy" (1941), Spike Jones's "Der Fuehrer's Face" (1942), and Louis Jordan's "G.I. Jive" (1944). These tunes were patriotic and silly. They were meant to boost the morale of soldiers. They were songs the whole family could enjoy. Pop stars in this period were not looking to rock the boat.

RACE RECORDS

Throughout the late 1940s, most mainstream record labels released a wide variety of songs. These included tunes that targeted returning World War II veterans. The soldiers enjoyed pop singers such as Bing Crosby, Patti Page, and Eileen Barton. None of these singers were at all provocative. Bing Crosby, for example, sang and acted in movies, where he portrayed priests, fathers, and other authority figures. However, mainstream record labels were not the only game in town. Small record labels such as Chess, Vee-Jay, and King Records cropped up too. These smaller labels produced "race records"—albums recorded by and marketed to African Americans. These records were the black popular music of the 1940s and the 1950s. If a listener put one of these records on the record player, he or she would have heard one of many musical styles, from R & B to gospel and jazz.

Some race records, such as gospel and jazz albums, offered clean, family-friendly material. Others had an edge. Many R & B singers, for example, sang about relationships gone sour, desperate men forced into violent situations, and racy love affairs. These songs were at odds with the pop songs of white singers who sang about the local drugstore and other conservative themes of daily life. The title of Muddy Waters's classic blues song "I'm Your Hoochie Coochie Man" (1954) refers to sexual prowess. This wasn't something listeners heard in a Bing Crosby tune. It was, however, big business. These albums sold like hotcakes to young, African American fans.

NEW SOUND FOR A NEW GENERATION

In the years after World War II, the United States experienced an

Muddy Waters's "I'm Your Hoochie Coochie Man" (1954) is among the Rock and Roll Hall of Fame's most influential songs. Waters's ability to make the slide guitar "sing" influenced musicians in many genres.

economic boom. This boom brought about a new era in radio broadcasting. Before the war, the nation's pop hits were played over a small group of national radio networks. After the war, listeners gained a cluster of smaller, independent, local radio stations. Some of these smaller stations were owned by African Americans. Other stations hired black disc jockeys (deejays) to play race records. Younger white audiences were intrigued by the new sounds on their radios. They had grown tired of listening to their parents' pop music and yearned for something new and fresh.

In those days, radio disc jockeys had a sort of secret, "underground" rapport (connection) with their listeners. Older black listeners disapproved of them, as did older white audiences. But white teens started turning the radio dial to stations playing race records. They wanted to sample the outrageous, sexy

Fats Domino knew how to get listeners rocking to his infectious beat. He sold more records in the 1950s than any other rock 'n' roll star except Elvis Presley. Domino's best-known hit is "Blueberry Hill" (1956).

lyrics. And then an interesting thing happened. Stations that played race records also started playing a new genre of music, a style that had evolved from R & B. This new genre was called rock 'n' roll.

THE ARCHITECTS OF ROCK

Early rock 'n' roll music came from blending a variety of race music, including blues and R & B. The first rock musicians, such as Fats Domino, Little Richard, Chuck Berry, and Ike Turner, were black. The music they made in the late 1940s and early 1950s wasn't labeled rock music in its day. Only later did historians realize that these were the first rumblings of rock. As

ROCK ALBUM NO. 1

Musicologists (people who study the history of music) don't agree on what the first rock album is. In 1949 Fats Domino recorded the song "The Fat Man," which some fans and scholars considered to be the first rock 'n' roll record. However, in 1951, the Kings of Rhythm—led by Jackie Brenston and Ike Turner—released the record "Rocket '88.'" Other people consider this to be the first true rock 'n' roll record.

When Elvis first came on the scene in the 1950s, television cameras filmed him only from the waist up. His sexy hip moves were considered inappropriate for viewers of the era. In this 1955 photo, he works a teen crowd into a frenzy.

> In Elvis, you have the blueprint for rock & roll.... Sexual liberation. Controversy. Changing the way people feel about the world.
> —BONO, 2011

Little Richard wrote in 2011, "A lot of people call me the architect of rock & roll. I don't call myself that, but I believe it's true."

White kids who listened to early rock 'n' roll records learned the slang and copied the dance moves that they saw in dance clubs and on TV shows. But some of these white kids did more than just mimic the dance moves and jargon. Some of them created their own spin on this music. They added a dash of country music to the mix, and wham! The first wave of white rock stars was born.

ROCK GOES MAINSTREAM

Elvis Presley was the first rock star to prove that rock wasn't just a passing fad. Through him, rock became part of the American pop music scene. In the 1950s, when Presley first hit the scene, the United States was a segregated nation. In many places, laws did not allow whites and blacks to eat at the same restaurants, use the same public bathrooms, stay in the same hotels, or go to the same schools. Because of this segregation and racism, many white audiences didn't feel comfortable idolizing a black rock singer. But Mississippi-born Presley was white. Presley's soulful vocals made him valuable to a record producer who was looking for the sexy appeal of black music but from a white singer. That record producer was Sam Phillips in Memphis, Tennessee. Phillips ran Sun Studio, where artists such as Johnny Cash and B. B. King also cut records.

In addition to his unique take on rock 'n' roll music, Presley's good looks, distinctive hairstyle, and flashy fashions also set him apart. Armed with a catchy sound, a cool look, and hip-swiveling dance moves, Elvis Presley was almost single-handedly responsible for placing rock music in the mainstream. Rock 'n' roll of the 1950s did have other stars, such as Jerry Lee Lewis, Buddy Holly, and Chuck Berry. However, Presley's star rose higher than anyone else's—and stayed there.

POP IDOLS

Most rock music of the 1950s was pop music. Many teens loved it because it championed disobedience and angst (a feeling of anxiety or dread), as well as sexual desire. In the late 1950s and the early 1960s, another type of pop music was gaining popularity. It was led by teen idols whose image was obedient and orderly. This was the first time that teen performers were at the forefront of popular American music.

These pop idols were clean-cut, and their lyrics did not touch on sexual matters the way rock music did. These pop songs occasionally spoke of teen drama, but not in the dramatic, over-the-top manner of rock. These pop songs addressed teen anxiety, in a sweet, pining way, full of innocent yearning. This was pop music that parents approved of.

With his boyish good looks and his easygoing ways, Paul Anka

Paul Anka began his career as a teen idol and has become a prolific songwriter. He has written hits such as "Diana" (1957) and "Lonely Boy" (1959) for himself as well as megahits for other stars such as "She's a Lady" (1971) for pop singer Tom Jones.

CAPTAIN PRESLEY

Elvis Presley's style was inspired by his favorite childhood superhero, Captain Marvel Jr. Like him, Presley wore capes and a hairdo called a pompadour. In the 1970s, after he was a rich star, he even gave out solid gold necklaces to friends. Each necklace had a lightning bolt, which was the symbol Captain Marvel Jr. wore on his chest.

was one of the most popular teen idols of the 1950s. He had a wholesome glow, singing songs of joy and romance. When he performed his first hit, "Diana" (1957), on the popular *Ed Sullivan Show*, fifteen-year-old Anka looked just like one of the clean-cut kids from the audience of teen fans. He had a vulnerability and nonthreatening charm that listeners—especially young females—found irresistible.

Bobby Darin was another teen pop idol of the late 1950s. Like Anka's songs, Darin's work was a big contrast to the rock music of that period. His biggest hit, "Mack the Knife" (1959), was originally written in 1928 for an operatic German musical called *The Threepenny Opera*.

Bobby Darin's career took off with "Splish Splash" (1958). He is said to have cowritten the song as a response to a bet that he couldn't come up with a song that started out with such silly words. The record sold more than one million copies.

GIRL STARS

Most of the pop idols of the late 1950s and the early 1960s were male. A few female pop singers did rise to the top of the charts. For example, Lesley Gore (RIGHT) recorded the hit song "It's My Party (I'll Cry If I Want To)" in 1963 when she was fifteen years old. Gore's songs—including "It's My Party," "Judy's Turn to Cry," and "You Don't Own Me" (all of which were released in 1963)—didn't inspire feelings of rebelliousness. Instead, they spoke to teens about their own anxieties.

The iconic British rock band the Beatles included, FROM LEFT, Paul McCartney, George Harrison, Ringo Starr, and John Lennon. The Beatles ushered in major changes to rock 'n' roll, including a shift from solo artists to groups and away from professional songwriters to bands writing their own material.

The song is about a serial killer nicknamed Mack the Knife because of his weapon of choice. Yet Darin sang the song in a jaunty, upbeat manner. It spent nine weeks at the No. 1 slot on the pop charts and won a Grammy Award for Darin that year. Darin's rhythmic delivery was so full of life and happiness that listeners quickly forgot that the song was about a murderer.

THE FIRST BOY BAND

Throughout the 1960s, a number of rock groups from the United Kingdom (UK) found success with American audiences. They included the Rolling Stones, Herman's Hermits, the Kinks, the Who, and many others. This wave of British musical talent is known as the British Invasion. And there was no bigger British import in the 1960s than the Beatles.

There were four Beatles—John Lennon, Paul McCartney, George Harrison, and Ringo Starr. Although they started out as scruffy rock 'n' roll musicians, the Beatles had a manager, Brian Epstein, who transformed their image, so that they seemed more clean-cut and

EUROPEAN ROCK ROYALTY

Like many boy bands that followed them, the Beatles were a big hit in Europe before U.S. audiences "discovered" them. The Fab Four (as the Beatles were known) became popular throughout Europe playing different clubs in 1961 and 1962.

family friendly. Megastars of pop, the Beatles unintentionally created the model for what would eventually come to be known as the boy band. Sure, the Beatles wrote their own songs and played their own instruments, and the same couldn't always be said for other boy bands. However, many of the boy bands since then, from the Jackson 5 to the Jonas Brothers, have followed the Beatles' model in other ways. For example, in every boy band since the Beatles, each of the members is adorable and nonthreatening, a professionally groomed and polished singer, and easily labeled. Even today, John Lennon is still remembered as "the smart one" and Paul McCartney as "the cute one."

George Harrison is remembered as "the quiet one," while Ringo Starr was "the goofy one."

In the early 1960s, the Beatles made hits such as "Love Me Do" (1962) and "She Loves You" (1963). The songs' simple but clever lyrics connected with the band's teen fan base. Then, from 1965 to 1970, the Beatles strayed from pure pop music into pure rock 'n' roll. As the band members got older and their lives became more complex, so did their music. The Beatles stopped being a boy band because they were no longer boys. ★

Nick Jonas LEFT was originally a solo performer, singing and acting in Broadway musicals in the early 2000s. In 2005 Nick and his brothers Kevin RIGHT and Joe CENTER signed with Columbia Records as a boy band called the Jonas Brothers, releasing their first single, "Mandy," in 2005.

BEACH BOY BAND

If one group could be said to be the Beatles' American contemporaries, that group would be the Beach Boys (ABOVE). From roughly 1962 until 1966, the Beach Boys' musical journey was similar to that of the Beatles. Both groups went from clean-cut boy band to artistically experimental trailblazers. Formed in 1961, the Beach Boys' original lineup consisted of the Wilson brothers—Brian, Carl, and Dennis— as well as their cousin Mike Love and their friend Al Jardine.

Known for their beautiful, intricate vocal harmonies, during the mid-1960s, the Beach Boys were America's most successful pop act. After 1966 the Beach Boys' bandleader, Brian Wilson, experienced drug problems, and the band's success declined in later years. However, at the peak of their popularity, the Beach Boys were the only group to rival the Beatles, both commercially and artistically.

MUST DOWNLOAD Playlist

FATS DOMINO
"The Fat Man," 1949

KINGS OF RHYTHM
"Rocket '88,'" 1951

MUDDY WATERS
"Hoochie Coochie Man," 1954

ELVIS PRESLEY
"That's All Right," 1954

PAUL ANKA
"Diana," 1957

BOBBY DARIN
"Mack the Knife," 1959

LESLEY GORE
"It's My Party," 1963

THE BEATLES
"I Want to Hold Your Hand," 1963

THE ROLLING STONES
"(I Can't Get No) Satisfaction," 1965

THE BEACH BOYS
"Good Vibrations," 1966

chapter 2 POP GOES Bubblegum

In this photo from 1968, Buddah Records producers Jerry Kasenetz LEFT and Jeff Katz RIGHT share a laugh about their success with bubblegum pop.

POP MUSIC DURING THE LATE 1960S AND THE EARLY 1970S WAS CRAFTED FOR THE YOUNGER SIBLINGS OF ROCK FANS.

The new breed of pop stars of this era often didn't write the songs they sang. Producer-songwriters did it for them. While rock groups were usually formed by the musicians themselves, pop groups were often brought together by record companies.

THE BIRTH OF BUBBLEGUM

With producers rather than musical artists controlling pop music, a new type of pop was bubbling to the surface. It was called bubblegum pop, and it was for kids. The first steady stream of bubblegum pop songs came in 1968. Some record labels started signing artists who sang bubblegum pop. . . and nothing else.

Two producers—Jerry Kasenetz and Jeff Katz—turned bubblegum into its own thing. In fact, Kasenetz and Katz came up with the term *bubblegum music*. Kids chew bubblegum, and this music was for kids. Kasenetz and Katz worked for a new label

The Archies cast of musical characters included, LEFT TO RIGHT, Betty, Archie, Jughead, Reggie, Veronica, and Jughead's faithful mutt, Hot Dog. One of the group's biggest hits was "Sugar, Sugar" (1969).

called Buddah Records. Buddah was a deliberate misspelling of the word *Buddha* (the main holy figure in the Buddhist religion).

Together Kasenetz and Katz were known as Super K Productions. Super K was like a hit factory. The Super K songwriting staff wrote songs quickly. Then Kasenetz, Katz, and their staff decided which artists would sing which songs.

One of the first bubblegum pop groups was a band called the 1910 Fruitgum Company. Super K released the band—named after a brand of chewing gum—on the Buddah label. Their biggest hit was

"Simon Says" (1968), a song whose lyrics explain the rules of the children's game Simon Says.

IN 'TOON

Super K's biggest competition was a group called the Archies. Like the 1910 Fruitgum Company, the Archies were a prefab group (short for *prefabricated*, or put together in advance). The producer Don Kirshner put the band together in 1968. The Archies didn't write their own material either. But the similarity to the 1910 Fruitgum Company ends

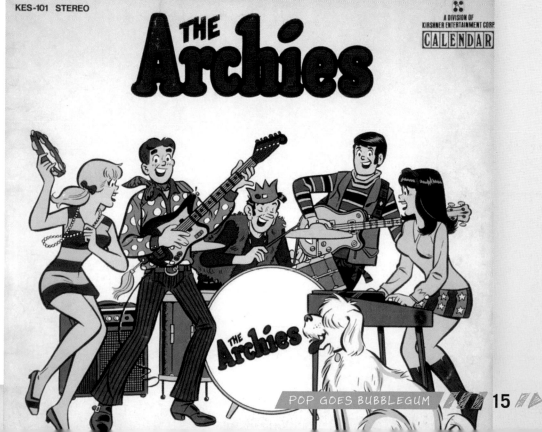

KES-101 STEREO

A DIVISION OF KIRSHNER ENTERTAINMENT CORP

CALENDAR

THE Archies

CASTING the STARS

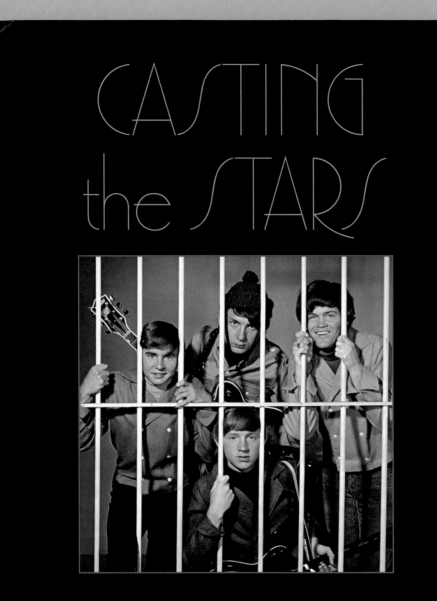

Many times, producers auditioned pop performers and cast them to fill certain roles, not unlike actors in a movie. This was definitely true of pop groups such as the Monkees (ABOVE), a late-1960s combo. The band's four members—Davy Jones, Mike Nesmith, Peter Tork, and Micky Dolenz—had never met until they started recording their first album, The Monkees (1966).

there. The 1910 Fruitgum Company was made up of real people. The Archies were a fictional band. Well, sort of.

The Archies were lead characters from the Archie series of comic books. They included clumsy redhead teen Archie Andrews; blonde do-gooder Betty Cooper; wealthy and jealous brunette Veronica Lodge; mean-spirited Reggie Mantle; and lazy clown Jughead Jones, who loves to eat. A group of professional musicians recorded songs as if they had been written by Archie and his friends. Fans never saw the people behind the music.

The Archies had a tie-in animated series on TV. At some point in the show, they would break out their musical instruments and play a tune. The Archies' single "Sugar, Sugar" won a gold record award in 1969 for selling more than six million copies. It was the No. 1 hit of that year.

A FAMILY THING

Teen pop groups made up of family members were a huge craze in the 1970s. These groups boasted an entire singing family. At the top of the musical heap stood the Jackson 5.

The Jackson 5—Jackie, Tito, Jermaine, Marlon, and

Michael—was the first African American bubblegum pop group. They were from Gary, Indiana. Their father, Joe Jackson, was a steel mill crane operator who played blues guitar in local clubs. Starting in 1962, Joe worked on turning his male children into a family music group. (The Jackson family also included three sisters, Rebbie, Janet, and La Toya.) They performed at local talent shows. Before long, two music professionals noticed the group—first, singer Gladys Knight and then Motown performer-producer Bobby Taylor. Motown was a recording studio in Detroit, Michigan, headed by Berry Gordy. Motown focused on African American artists. Gordy knew that with the Jackson 5, Motown could

put its own spin on bubblegum. As historian James Porter wrote, "There had never been an African-American act marketed towards the... white teenybopper [teen] market. Berry Gordy and the Jacksons saw an opening and rolled right through."

The Jackson 5 boasted a behind-the-scenes team of talented producer-songwriters (called the Corporation) who worked hard to create an energetic, fun-loving image for the group. Their safe, G-rated image set them apart from other African American R & B, which was racier and aimed at adults. The American public loved the group's first album, **Diana Ross Presents the Jackson 5** (1969). The release made it to the Top 5

of the Billboard Hot 100. Four of their singles during the following year—"I Want You Back," "ABC," "The Love You Save," and "I'll Be There"—each hit No. 1. In fact, this made the Jackson 5 the first black male pop group to achieve four consecutive No. 1 hits.

THE OSMONDS

From the western United States came another family group. Originally called the Osmond Brothers, the Osmonds were a large Mormon family from Utah. They regularly performed on a popular TV variety show hosted by crooner Andy

LEFT TO RIGHT: Tito, Marlon, Jackie, Michael, and Jermaine Jackson perform in London in 1972. The Jackson 5 appealed equally to white and black audiences.

BUBBLEGUM R & B

The Jackson 5 was the first pop group to fuse bubblegum and R & B. But they certainly weren't the last. They inspired future bubblegum R&B acts, such as the Ponderosa Twins Plus One, New Edition, and 'N Sync.

Williams. The group included brothers Alan, Wayne, Merrill, and Jay Osmond. (Later, Donny and Jimmy Osmond joined the group.)

The Osmond Brothers followed the pattern set earlier by wholesome boy singers such as Paul Anka. They were young and talented and sang cheerful, upbeat songs. The Osmonds were also influenced by the Jackson 5. For example, they dressed in flashy, stylish clothes. Their dance moves were synchronized (coordinated neatly)—just like those of the Jackson 5. But on songs such as "One Bad Apple" (1971), the Osmonds used a toned-down version of the R & B sass of Jackson 5 songs.

While he was performing with his brothers, Donny Osmond also pursued a solo career. During that time, he covered (recorded his own version of) pop hits such as "Puppy Love" (1972). Then, in 1973, his sister, Marie Osmond, took off on her own solo career. Marie felt that country music spoke more to her. She mixed it with a pop sound, and the result was country pop. Marie had her biggest hit with the 1973 single "Paper Roses," a cover of a song originally recorded in 1960 by Anita Bryant.

The following year, Marie teamed up with her teen idol brother Donny to record a pair of duets. The first duet, "I'm Leaving It All Up to You," was a Top 20 Country hit. The siblings had fun performing together in their live shows, and the fun was infectious. Donnie and Marie Osmond teamed up again in 1976 to host a TV variety show titled *Donnie & Marie*. The series lasted three seasons.

The Osmond Brothers offered a scrubbed-clean take on the R & B groove in their pop hits of the 1970s. Donny Osmond FRONT CENTER went on to a successful solo career. He continues to be active in musical theater and radio.

The Partridge Family was another popular family-based pop group of the 1970s. The group's biggest hit was "I Think I Love You" (1970). Many fans followed the group on its popular TV show, The Partridge Family.

THE PARTRIDGE FAMILY

The Osmonds were a real-life pop family. The Partridge Family band was anything but. The Partridge Family was a silly, lighthearted combination of the Monkees (a fictional pop group), the Osmonds, and the Scooby-Doo gang. (Scooby and friends traveled the United States in search of adventure, and so did the Partridges.) Like The Archies in the late 1960s, the Partridge Family was made up of actors playing the roles of pop stars on a TV show by the same name. The live-action television series The Partridge Family (1970–1974) was about widowed mom Shirley Partridge (played by Broadway and film actress Shirley Jones) and her five children. The TV family toured the country in their bus with manager Reuben Kincaid (Dave Madden). Teen heart-throb Keith Partridge, played by David Cassidy, was considered the cute one. His younger, sarcastic

brother (Danny Bonaduce) was the funny one. Older sister Laurie (Susan Dey) was the pretty one.

The Partridges boasted a spin-off comic book and a line of children's mystery books. Meanwhile, the Osmonds had a tie-in animated TV series, produced by cartoon studio Rankin/Bass. This studio had also produced the Beatles' tie-in animated TV series. All these products were meant to appeal to children and tweens. However, handsome teenage boy singers such as Keith Partridge, Donny Osmond, and Michael Jackson also won over teen girl fans.

TIME FOR CHANGE

After 1972 the first wave of bubblegum pop faded. Teenage girls focused their attention on a new crop of teen idols. Successful bubblegum pop acts from this period included Swedish pop sensation ABBA; teen idol Leif Garrett; Scottish pop group the Bay City Rollers; and Shaun Cassidy, the half brother of the Partridge Family's David Cassidy.

Bubblegum pop was on its way out. But pop music itself wasn't dead. It had simply given way to something called disco.

WHEN DISCO WAS KING

In the early 1970s, black and gay dance clubs led the New York underground party scene. Favorite performers were often female. This was a contrast to rock 'n' roll, where performers were mostly white heterosexual males. From this underground scene, a new style of music began to emerge at discotheques (dance clubs). Funk, soul, and Latin beats inspired this music.

By 1973 the word *discotheque* was shortened to disco. The term described clubs that played records of music that was easy to dance to. In September 1973, journalist Vince Aletti wrote the first article about disco for *Rolling Stone*. With this type of press coverage, the music went mainstream. Young adults and teens who had left bubblegum pop behind turned to disco.

Disco music was fun. It appealed to many kinds of people, whether black, gay, straight, Latino, male, or female. Disco clubs borrowed hairstyles and fashions from the hippie movement of the late 1960s. The clubs were home to psychedelic (colorful, dreamlike) lighting, free-form dance moves, and outrageous costumes. Disco music also borrowed the hippies' peaceful, "all-are-welcome-here" vibe. Disco became so trendy that even old-time performers such as Ethel Merman jumped on the bandwagon. With her booming voice, Merman belted out disco versions of classic Broadway tunes

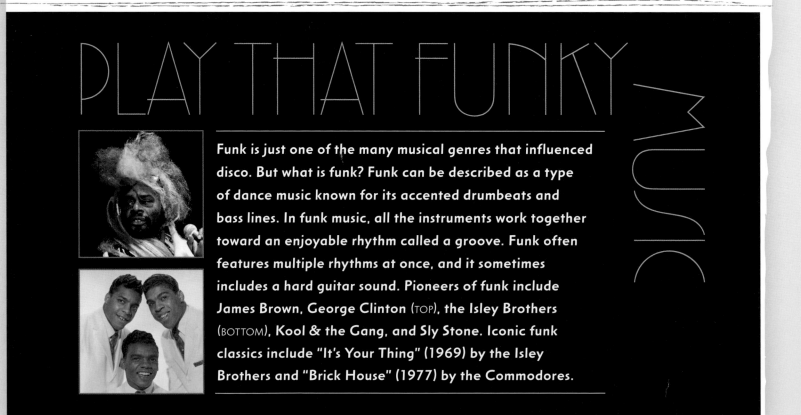

PLAY THAT FUNKY MUSIC

Funk is just one of the many musical genres that influenced disco. But what is funk? Funk can be described as a type of dance music known for its accented drumbeats and bass lines. In funk music, all the instruments work together toward an enjoyable rhythm called a groove. Funk often features multiple rhythms at once, and it sometimes includes a hard guitar sound. Pioneers of funk include James Brown, George Clinton (TOP), the Isley Brothers (BOTTOM), Kool & the Gang, and Sly Stone. Iconic funk classics include "It's Your Thing" (1969) by the Isley Brothers and "Brick House" (1977) by the Commodores.

DISCO'S FIRST HIT

on her 1979 Disco Album, which she recorded in her early seventies.

LEADERS OF THE (SUNSHINE) BAND

KC and the Sunshine Band was a pop group that moved to the disco beat. The band's members were black and white, male and female. They were just as diverse as their audience. Harry Wayne "K. C." Casey and Richard Finch formed the band in 1973. KC and the Sunshine Band didn't have to wait long for their first hit. "Rock Your Baby" (1974) was an international success and an early disco smash. The band wasn't successful in the United

States until 1975. That year they released their second album, **KC and the Sunshine Band**. The album had instant disco classics such as "Get Down Tonight" and "That's the Way (I Like It)." By 1980 the group had earned nine Grammy nominations and had won three awards.

DISCO'S ROYAL FAMILY

If disco had kings, they would have been three of the Gibb brothers,

KC and the Sunshine Band were a hot disco group who hit their peak in the 1970s and the early 1980s. They retired until disco became popular again in the 1990s.

> "We were never consciously writing disco music.
>
> We thought we were just writing pop songs you could dance to, like black American R & B, Otis Redding, Stax [Records], Sam and Dave."
>
> —Robin Gibb, 2009

Barry, Robin, and Maurice. (Younger brother Andy Gibb was a solo performer.) The Gibbs were born on the Isle of Man, an island off the coast of England. In 1958 the Gibb family moved to Australia. In the early 1960s, the three brothers began performing as a singing group. Calling themselves the Rattlesnakes, they went through various name changes and eventually settled on the Bee Gees (which stood for Brothers Gibb).

The Bee Gees rose to the top of the new disco scene. In 1977 they sang several songs for the sound track of the hit film *Saturday Night Fever*, which featured actor John Travolta in a star-making role. With the *Saturday Night Fever* songs, the Bee Gees became the band behind the most popular music style of the 1970s. With their well-known high-pitched voices, they would forever be associated with disco through hit songs such as "Stayin' Alive," "Night Fever," and "How Deep Is Your Love," all released in 1977.

The Bee Gees had an enormous success with the 1979 album **Spirits Having Flown.** The album sold 20 million copies and boasted three No. 1 singles. Even in the twenty-first century, the Bee Gees remain one of the top vocal acts of all time. According

LEFT TO RIGHT Robin, Barry, and Maurice Gibb were at the forefront of the disco craze. The phenomenal success of their **Saturday Night Fever** sound track (1977) brought disco into the mainstream.

to the Rock and Roll Hall of Fame website, they rank sixth on the all-time best-sellers list, just behind Elvis Presley, the Beatles, Michael Jackson, Garth Brooks, and Paul McCartney.

If the Bee Gees were the kings of disco, disco's queen was Donna Summer. Born LaDonna Gaines in Boston, Donna Summer grew up with a love of music. By the early 1970s, she was performing in the European tour of the Broadway musical Hair. In Germany she met a pair of producers-songwriters who helped her create her first No. 1 disco hit, "Love to Love You Baby" (1975). Summer's racy performance of that song was inspired by legendary actress Marilyn Monroe, who was famous for combining innocence and sexiness. In fact, many disco songs are sexy, and this was one of the elements that set them apart from other types of pop songs. Some of Donna Summer's other hit songs of the late 1970s and the early 1980s include "Last Dance" (1978), "Hot Stuff" (1979), and "She Works Hard for the Money" (1983).

DISCO SUCKS! (OR DOES IT?)

By the early 1980s, disco performers such as the Bee Gees, Donna Summer, and KC and the Sunshine Band found themselves out of fashion. What had happened?

As one music critic wrote in 2002, "By 1979, when disco had become an industry generating $4 billion annually and there were an estimated 15,000 discotheques in the nation, a backlash was inevitable." In fact, by the late 1970s, rock 'n' roll fans were burning disco records. And people began wearing T-shirts that read "Disco Sucks!" The public was ready for the next big thing. ★

♪ MUST DOWNLOAD Playlist

THE MONKEES
"Daydream Believer," 1967

1910 FRUITGUM COMPANY
"Simon Says," 1968

THE ISLEY BROTHERS
"It's Your Thing," 1969

THE ARCHIES
"Sugar, Sugar," 1969

THE JACKSON 5
"ABC," 1970

THE OSMONDS
"One Bad Apple," 1970

THE PARTRIDGE FAMILY
"I Think I Love You," 1970

HUES CORPORATION
"Rock the Boat," 1974

KC AND THE SUNSHINE BAND
"Get Down Tonight," 1975

BEE GEES
"Stayin' Alive," 1977

GLORIA GAYNOR
"I Will Survive," 1978

chapter 3

MTV GENERATION

With the launch of Music Television (MTV) in 1981, the term video jockey, or VJ, came into the English language. The station's first VJs were, LEFT TO RIGHT, Alan Hunter, Martha Quinn, Mark Goodman, Nina Blackwood, and J. J. Jackson.

BY THE EARLY 1980S, DISCO HAD COME TO A SCREECHING HALT. THE RECORD INDUSTRY WAS IN A SLUMP.

Record executives weren't sure what audiences wanted. At this time, VCRs (videocassette recorders) were brand new. People began to experiment with video technology. Many rock 'n' roll stars, such as the Rolling Stones and the Doors, had already produced short music videos during the late 1960s and into the 1970s. These videos were mostly promotional.

Meanwhile, the late-night NBC show *Album Tracks* (which ran after *Saturday Night Live*) had begun showing some music videos. Cable television stations were also becoming more common. Bob Pittman, head of programming for Warner-Amex Satellite Entertainment Company, wanted to put together a "video radio station." This new television network would consist entirely of music videos, music news, and other music-related programming. It would run twenty-four hours a day, seven days a week. MTV (Music Television, logo at right) was born.

MTV at the MOVIES

The Beatles, along with the director Richard Lester, made a few very popular films in the 1960s. These films included *A Hard Day's Night* (1964) (LEFT) and *Help* (1965). The Beatles both acted and played songs throughout the films. The movies had loose plots to allow time for the musical sequences. Their rapid pacing and irreverent tone later influenced MTV.

DEATH OF A STAR

The song "Video Killed the Radio Star" (1979) predicted that Americans would rely less and less on radio for music. After MTV, Americans asked themselves, Why just listen to performers on the radio when you can see them on TV too? That was the key to MTV's appeal in its early years.

LADIES AND GENTLEMEN, ROCK 'N' ROLL

At 12:01 A.M., on August 1, 1981, America watched the launch of MTV. First, viewers saw footage of the launch of the space shuttle Columbia, while a voice said, "Ladies and gentlemen, rock 'n' roll." Then viewers saw MTV's first music video of the song "Video Killed the Radio Star" (1979) by a rock group called the Buggles.

Only a few thousand people saw MTV's debut on that warm August night. That was because only a few thousand homes were wired to receive the station. Even viewers in New York City, MTV's headquarters, couldn't watch MTV. In the early days of MTV, sometimes the screen would go black between videos. This was because staff at MTV were putting a new tape into the VCR. Early MTV was low-budget, but it would soon expand its reach. Most homes in the United States—and eventually the world—would soon be MTV-friendly.

The Buggles were a British duo. Trevor Horn RIGHT sang vocals and played guitar, while Geoff Downes LEFT provided keyboards. The two performed "Video Killed the Radio Star" on MTV's first televised video.

MJTV

By 1983 MTV was on its way to becoming a major cable network. It produced a series of ads featuring major rock and pop stars. The first one starred Mick Jagger of the Rolling Stones, saying, "I want my MTV!"

Like mainstream radio stations, MTV "video jockeys," or VJs, played videos featuring mostly Caucasian rockers such as Rod Stewart and Adam Ant. Many of

MTV's early videos came from England, where music videos had been popular for a longer time. Most of the British music videos featured white performers too. MTV did show videos by a few black artists, such as reggae performer Eddy Grant and R & B singer Tina Turner.

But the network ignored huge talents such as Rick James, who had a major funk-R & B hit with his song "Super Freak" in 1981.

James couldn't get MTV to play his "Super Freak" music video. MTV claimed the video was too edgy and

Rick James was a talented singer-songwriter and record producer with a funky beat. He formed his first band with future Steppenwolf bass player Nick St. Nicholas in the mid-1960s.

Tina Turner got her start with husband Ike Turner as a member of the Ike & Tina Turner Revue. Tina went on to a successful solo career, launching her first solo album, **Tina Turns the Country On!**, in 1974.

> [Michael Jackson] opened the minds of people about music. He...helped with segregation.
>
> His music did that and not a lot of people can say that.
>
> —Justin Timberlake, 2011

VIDEO VISUALS

Because of music videos, looks began to matter more than ever in the world of music. Suddenly, it was extremely important for pop stars to be photogenic (look physically attractive in photos) so they would look good in a music video. Before music videos became popular, a fan might see a pop star from the fortieth row of a concert arena. But on TV, they could see their favorite artist up close. And if artists didn't pay attention to looks, it might mean that their albums wouldn't sell as well.

over-the-top. So James waged a crusade to get MTV to feature more artists of color, and ABC's *Nightline* featured the story on television.

During this same time, Michael Jackson's album *Thriller* (1982) was a record-smashing success. The songs on this album contained elements of both R & B and pop. He was considered a crossover artist, since audiences of all races and backgrounds loved his music and were buying the album. Many people wondered why viewers couldn't watch Jackson's videos on MTV as well.

MTV's cofounder, Les Garland, thought they should be able to. He decided to air the video for Jackson's song "Billie Jean," even though it was an R & B song and didn't fit MTV's all-rock formula. "Billie Jean" blew away the channel's viewers. In the video, Michael Jackson dances across a larger-than-life cityscape straight out of an old Broadway musical. Every time his body touches a solid object—a floor tile or a lamppost—it causes that object to light up. Everything about "Billie Jean" was of such high quality (and the song was so popular) that the network had to overrule its earlier decision to show only rock videos. Who cared that "Billie Jean" wasn't rock? It was good, and that was all that mattered. "Billie Jean" opened the door for Michael Jackson and for other artists of color at MTV.

Michael Jackson BACK CENTER in the zombie sequence from the famous *Thriller* (1982) music video. This video merged dance and vocals in an impressive short film. It set a new standard for music videos, which until that time had not been based in filmic storytelling.

THE PRINCE of POP

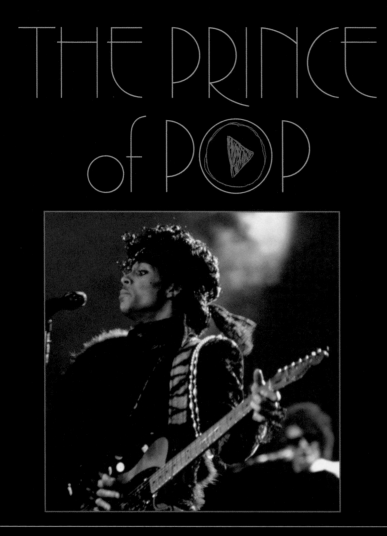

Michael Jackson wasn't the only African American pop icon of the 1980s. Another influential star was Prince (ABOVE). He was born Prince Rogers Nelson in 1958 in Minneapolis, Minnesota. His sixth studio album, **Purple Rain** (1984), was a monster hit, selling more than 10 million copies in the United States. Prince also starred in the movie *Purple Rain*, which was released that same year. Over the years, he has shown great musical inventiveness, often blending together funk, pop, rock, and folk. He frequently writes music for, produces, and plays many of the instruments on his own recordings. Prince has also been a huge influence on more recent pop stars, such as Ke$ha.

Jackson's next video on the network, "Beat It," blew that door off its hinges. Here, Jackson mixed his R & B style with a guitar solo from rock god Eddie Van Halen. Both R & B and rock 'n' roll fans loved the song and the video and bought *Thriller*. It became one of the top-selling albums of all time. After the success of the *Beat It* video, MTV began playing Michael Jackson videos over and over again.

Jackson's next video—the title track of his **Thriller** album— was a fourteen-minute short film that spoofed horror movies of the past. It was directed by A-list filmmaker John Landis (*An American Werewolf in London*, 1981). It included exciting choreography, monster makeup, and even a rap performed (in voiceover) by horror movie legend Vincent Price. Also, it was the first video that gave MTV a huge ratings spike every time MTV showed it. Usually, the network would average a rating of 1.2 (roughly 1.5 million adult viewers age 18–49) for a 24-hour period. On days when MTV played "Thriller," the rating would jump to an 8 or a 10. MTV could have retitled itself "MJTV," or "Michael Jackson TV."

Through Jackson's videos, the network's popularity soared. MTV began to show more videos by black artists. Soon, videos by performers such as Prince started regularly appearing on the network.

THE GIRL AND HER MATERIAL

Madonna was the most powerful female pop icon of the 1980s. She was the first artist to really use MTV to establish her popularity. Born in Michigan in 1958 as Madonna Louise Veronica Ciccone, she moved to New York City to study with the Alvin Ailey and Pearl Lang dance companies. In November 1982, her dance single "Everybody" reached the top of the dance charts. In 1983 Madonna's self-titled first album debuted, selling almost 10 million copies worldwide. Her music video for "Borderline" also premiered that year. With that video, TV audiences put a face to Madonna's name, and her image became as important as her music.

Girls all over the world began to copy Madonna's look. They put on cropped lace tops, revealing underwear, and fingerless gloves, drawing a beauty spot just above the top lip. In September 1984, Madonna performed the song "Like a Virgin" on MTV's first Video Music Awards show. In November 1984, her second album, also named *Like a Virgin*, reached No.1 on the U.S. music charts. The album made Madonna a major star all over the world.

Madonna performed her hit song "Like a Virgin" in a trademark mix of lacy lingerie, religious crosses, and Boy Toy belt buckle at the first MTV Video Music Awards in 1984. The next year, she earned positive reviews playing the quirky character Susan in Desperately Seeking Susan, her third movie role.

DANCE-POP DIVA

Madonna was a pioneer in the musical subgenre of dance-pop. Dance-pop is pop music that's specifically created to be played in clubs and danced to. With its danceable rhythms and strong beats, dance-pop has become more and more popular over the years. And while Madonna didn't create dance-pop, she popularized it. She blazed the trail for other dance-pop icons such as Janet Jackson, Britney Spears, and Katy Perry.

Madonna is best known for her provocative stage persona. In her videos and live shows, she has always worn exciting outfits. One of her most famous getups was a conical bra designed by French fashion designer Jean Paul Gaultier. She wore this eye-popping outfit for her 1990 Blond Ambition Tour. She also sings openly about female sexual desire and creates sexy videos for her songs, sometimes causing controversy.

In a pop music career that has lasted more than thirty years, Madonna has outlasted many of her contemporaries from the 1980s. She remains popular as both a recording artist and as a live performer. Madonna changed the way pop music thought of women. She proved they can be sassy, sexy, smart, and strong all at once.

THE RETURN OF BUBBLEGUM

As Madonna was hitting the top of the pop charts, a new boy band was riding to fame. New Edition was a group of

New Edition caught the attention of producer Maurice Starr in 1982. That year the group came in second at a talent show run by Starr. He took them into the studio the very next day to record **Candy Girl** (1983), their first album.

African American kids from Boston. The group consisted of Bobby Brown, Ralph Tresvant, Ricky Bell, Michael Bivins, and Ronnie DeVoe. They blended bubblegum pop and soul. They were also easily labeled, not unlike the Beatles or the Partridge Family. For example, Bobby Brown was the "bad boy," and Ralph Tresvant was the "cute one." New Edition's first album, 1983's **Candy Girl**, went to No. 1 on the R & B singles chart in the United States.

New Edition's producer, Maurice Starr, brought bubblegum boy bands back to the top of the charts in the 1980s and the early 1990s. In 1984 Starr founded a group called New Kids on the Block, shortly after he parted ways with New Edition. The New Kids—Donnie Wahlberg, Danny Wood, Joey McIntyre, and brothers Jordan Knight and Jonathan Knight—released their self-titled debut album in 1986. Jordan was the "cute one," Donnie was the "bad boy," and Jonathan was the "shy one." Almost all the songs in the group's first album were written by Starr himself. That album wasn't very popular. But **Hangin' Tough**, their 1988 follow-up record, boasted a slicker sound and more radio-ready lyrics. **Hangin' Tough** sold 8

million copies. Five songs from the album entered the Billboard Top 10, including the funk-influenced title track and the ballad "I'll Be Loving You (Forever)." Throughout 1988 and 1989, the New Kids on the Block were the hot new boy band.

By 1991 the New Kids on the Block had become the highest-paid entertainers of the year, beating out such heavyweights as Michael Jackson and Madonna. This was

Boy band New Kids on the Block pose in a photo taken at the height of their career in the late 1980s. Like New Edition, the members of New Kids were from Boston and shared Maurice Starr as their producer.

thanks to their global stardom. It was also due to the mountain of merchandise that young female fans could buy. If a fan already owned all the New Kids on the Block albums, there were always comic books, dolls, bedsheets, lunch boxes, and more.

The title track from the New Kids' 1990 album **Step by Step** was their biggest hit to date. But as their teen fans got older, the band's white-hot star began to cool. Over the next couple of years, their album sales dropped. In 1994 they renamed themselves NKOTB. That same year, they released the album **Face the Music**. This album was meant to convince fans that the former New Kids had become mature adults. They wrote many of its songs themselves. But **Face the Music** failed to make a dent, and NKOTB disbanded in June 1994.

SHOPPING
MALL TOUR

Female singers were also part of the renewed interest in bubblegum pop. As New Kids on the Block was gaining fame, Tiffany Darwish was gaining ground. Known simply as Tiffany, she burst onto the pop music scene in 1987 with her chart-topping, self-titled debut album. That album had her first hit song, a cover of the song "I Think We're Alone Now." (The song was first recorded twenty years earlier by Tommy James & the Shondells.) That same year, Tiffany made a bold, smart move. Realizing that her fans were mostly teenage

Teen idol Tiffany performs at a mall during her 1987 shopping mall tour across the United States. At first, her mall appearances were not well attended. But as her fame grew, so did the crowds who came to see her.

POP GODDESSES

Tiffany and Debbie Gibson (LEFT) each had a wholesome, respectable vibe. They sang bubblegum songs about romance and longing. But they never touched subjects such as sexuality. Neither pop goddess was at all controversial. Coming onto the scene after edgier pop stars such as Madonna and Prince, they reminded listeners of the family-friendly bubblegum pop that had been popular in the late 1960s and the early 1970s.

girls—and that teen girls hang out at the mall—Tiffany and her managers decided to stage her concerts in the malls. Tiffany was very successful from 1987 until 1989.

Tiffany's pop rival was Debbie Gibson. Like Tiffany, Gibson was a teen pop queen who had two No. 1 hits on the Billboard charts. One of these hits was "Foolish Beat" from her 1988 album **Out of the Blue**. The other was "Lost in Your Eyes" from her album **Electric Youth** (1989). When "Foolish Beat" came out, Gibson became the first teenager to write, produce, and sing on a U.S. No. 1 hit single. She was only seventeen years old. ★

♪ MUST DOWNLOAD *Playlist*

THE BUGGLES
"Video Killed the Radio Star," 1979

RICK JAMES
"Super Freak," 1981

MICHAEL JACKSON
"Thriller," 1982

ADAM ANT
"Goody Two Shoes," 1982

NEW EDITION
"Candy Girl," 1983

PRINCE
"When Doves Cry," 1984

MADONNA
"Material Girl," 1985

TIFFANY
"I Think We're Alone Now," 1987

DEBBIE GIBSON
"Lost in Your Eyes," 1989

NEW KIDS ON THE BLOCK
"I'll Be Loving You (Forever)," 1989

4 POP GOES THE Millennium

The Backstreet Boys were
popular in Europe long before
the boy band made it big in the
United States. The band was
put together through auditions
organized by producer Lou
Pearlman in the early 1990s.

AS BUBBLEGUM POP FANS GET OLDER, THEY USUALLY MOVE TO OTHER TYPES OF MUSIC.

As a result, the bands that they once liked fade away. New pop groups take their place. In the mid-1990s, New Kids on the Block and Tiffany became less popular as their fans grew up. Younger fans were eager for the next big pop star.

The newer, emerging pop stars were different from the ones who came before. These new stars often combined pop with other musical genres, such as R & B and hip-hop. Bubblegum pop was making a huge comeback, but this wasn't the bubblegum pop of previous generations. It was something new, something different.

LARGER THAN LIFE

The Backstreet Boys (also known by the initials BSB) came on the scene in the mid-1990s. They were an R & B-influenced bubblegum pop group that borrowed some of their style and looks from the New Kids on the Block. The Backstreet Boys had five members—A. J. McLean, Brian Littrell, Nick Carter, Kevin Richardson, and Howie Dorough. The band was founded by Lou Pearlman. Pearlman was a wealthy businessperson when he decided to enter the music industry. He took the band's name from the Backstreet flea market in Orlando, Florida.

The band first performed at Orlando's Sea World in May 1993. After that, its members perfected their skills at amusement parks and shopping malls all over the United States. The BSB's singing sound was a combination of new jack swing, dance-pop, and hip-hop. U.S. radio stations ignored the band, so it began a tour of Europe. European audiences loved them. Their first album, **The Backstreet Boys** (1995), was a smash hit overseas.

The BSB didn't have their first U.S. hit until two years later, with the American release of the single "Quit Playing Games (With My Heart)" (1997). It was an immediate success both in the United States and in Europe (where it had been released the previous year). The group's members had been practicing and performing their hearts out for four years. Yet the press called the band an overnight sensation.

THE BIG VOICE

As a child in the early 1990s, Christina Aguilera could sing like music legends Ella Fitzgerald and Etta James. Some called her "the

Pop music fans first heard Christina Aguilera's big voice in 1990 on the Star Search program. She signed her first record contract after recording "Reflection," a song from the animated film Mulan (1998).

The ORLANDO DREAM FACTORY

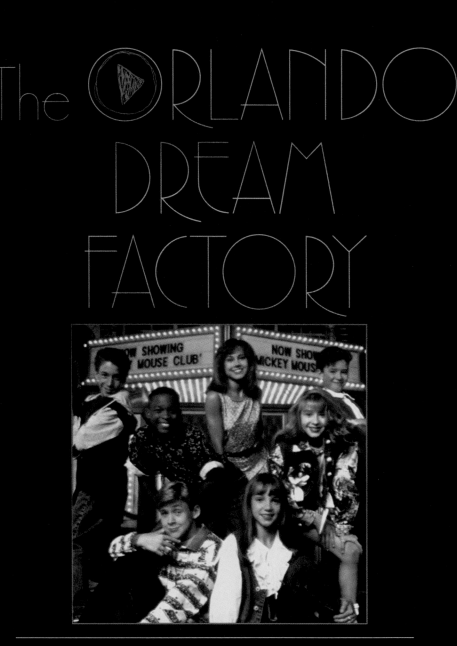

While the Backstreet Boys' career was ramping up, a whole new generation of pop stars was getting its start through television. The All-New Mickey Mouse Club, which ran from 1989 to 1994, was a modern version of a famed children's TV show from the 1950s. Any performer who appeared on the All-New Mickey Mouse Club had to be able to sing, dance, and act. The show was taped in Orlando, adding to that city's reputation as a pop music hub. And the cast just happened to include the future pop superstars Britney Spears (BOTTOM RIGHT), Justin Timberlake (TOP RIGHT), Christina Aguilera (MIDDLE RIGHT), and J. C. Chasez.

little girl with the big voice." Post-Mickey Mouse, her big break as a singer came with the 1998 animated Disney film Mulan. Aguilera was hired to sing "Reflection," a thoughtful tune from the movie's sound track. Only seventeen at the time, she impressed listeners with her powerful pipes. The next year, she released her own self-titled debut album. One song from that album, "Genie in a Bottle" (1999), gave Aguilera her first No.1 hit. "Genie" was a light dance-pop song. Her later albums had more serious songs such as "Hurt" (2006). This song deals with the pain of losing a loved one. "Beautiful," from Aguilera's album **Stripped** (2002), is a self-esteem anthem. The song encourages listeners to embrace who they are, even if they're not considered part of society's mainstream. To emphasize this, the music video for the song makes explicit references to gay people, people of color, transvestites, and victims of bullying. Aguilera, whose father is from Ecuador, has also embraced who she is. She explored her Latin roots with the Spanish-language album **Mi Reflejo (My Reflection)**, which was released in 2000. As of this writing, in addition to being a top pop star, Christina Aguilera is also one of the judges on The Voice, a popular TV singing competition.

OOPS

Not all female pop stars of the 1990s had something serious to say. Some of them, like Britney Spears, were content just having fun. In 1998 she released her debut album, **One More Time**. To listeners, Spears was a bubblegum pop princess with a hint of something naughty just beneath the surface.

Along with Christina Aguilera, the Backstreet Boys, and others, Britney Spears revived bubblegum pop in the late 1990s. Yet her style was also influenced by pop stars such as Madonna and Janet Jackson. Like them, Britney wears provocative, over-the-top costumes in her music videos and in live shows. And like them, she has a raspy, sultry singing voice.

In the early 2000s, Spears was ready to shed her teen pop image and to show the world that she was growing up. Her 2001 song "I'm Not a Girl, Not Yet a Woman" announced this loud and clear. That song came from her album **Britney** (2001), on which she cowrote five of the songs. The album aimed to prove that Spears was more than a bubblegum artist. For example, the song "I'm a Slave 4 U" is a pulsating funk number influenced by Prince. Spears's 2003 album **In the Zone** put even more distance between her and her bubblegum past. This album had songs such as the futuristic dance-pop hit "Toxic." Both **Britney** and **In the Zone** showed a pop star who was growing as an artist. She was experimenting with other musical styles and with a wide range of sounds.

Over the next several years, Spears battled problems in her personal life, including drug addiction. In her sixth album **Circus** (2008), she sang about the mistakes she'd made and about the triumphs and tragedies in her life. With her Femme Fatale Tour in 2011, Spears's fans saw her as a pro who had conquered her demons.

Pop princess Britney Spears has navigated the transition from teen idol to adult pop icon very successfully. In fact, Forbes magazine listed her as the third-highest-paid musician of 2011–2012.

> I have really strong morals, and just because I look sexy on the cover of Rolling Stone doesn't mean I'm a naughty girl.
>
> —Britney Spears, 1999

NO STRINGS

Teen pop sensation 'N Sync came on the scene in the late 1990s. Like the Backstreet Boys, the band was formed in Orlando. And they had the same force behind them: Lou Pearlman. He sent the band members—Justin Timberlake, J. C. Chasez, Chris Kirkpatrick, Joey Fatone, and Lance Bass—to Europe for experience. The time in Europe worked out even better than Pearlman could have dreamed. While it had taken five years for the Backstreet Boys to hit it big, it took 'N Sync only half as long to reach global fame.

'N Sync's singles "I Want You Back" (1996) and "Tearin' Up My Heart (1997) quickly became huge

hits throughout Europe. Then, in the summer of 1998, the Backstreet Boys had to back out of a TV concert. 'N Sync was tapped as their replacement. The special was a hit, and word of mouth spread about 'N Sync. By late August, their first album (*'N Sync*, which had been out since March) hit the top 10.

Soon 'N Sync was outselling the Backstreet Boys. 'N Sync's album *Celebrity* (2001) hit sales of 1.9 million in its first week of sales, beating out the first-week sales (1.1 million) of the Backstreet Boys' 1999 album, *Millennium*. And, 'N Sync's album *No Strings Attached* held the record for all-time best-selling preorders of a CD at Amazon.com when it came out in March 2000.

For a while, it seemed as though

Attached to cables, 'N Sync flies off the stage during a sold-out performance in Las Vegas to promote the group's **No Strings Attached** (2000) album.

'N Sync would last forever. Riding high into early 2002, the group saw *Celebrity* become the second-fastest-selling album of all time. But later that year, after a huge stadium tour, the group announced that it was taking a break. Justin Timberlake released his first solo album, *Justified*, that year. His shift from boy band member to successful solo artist marked the beginning of the end for 'N Sync. The break lasted until 2007, when Lance Bass announced that the group had split up. ★

A PINCH OF SPICE

In the late 1990s, the Spice Girls (ABOVE) briefly hit it big as a major dance-pop act. The members of the British girl group were Victoria Beckham (formerly Adams) (SECOND FROM RIGHT), Melanie Brown (CENTER), Emma Bunton (SECOND FROM LEFT), Melanie Chisholm (FAR LEFT), and Geri Halliwell (FAR RIGHT). They released their debut single, "Wannabe," in 1996. The singers got their stage names (Posh Spice, Scary Spice, Baby Spice, Sporty Spice, and Ginger Spice, respectively) from a British magazine. As with the bubblegum acts of the late 1960s and the early 1970s, the Spice Girls were masterminded by a producer—Simon Fuller. He also created the British television series Pop Idol and its U.S. equivalent, American Idol.

♪ MUST DOWNLOAD Playlist

SPICE GIRLS
"Wannabe," 1996

HANSON
"MMMBop," 1997

BACKSTREET BOYS
"Quit Playing Games (with My Heart)," 1997

BRITNEY SPEARS
"...Baby One More Time," 1998

RICKY MARTIN
"Livin' La Vida Loca," 1998

JENNIFER LOPEZ
"If You Had My Love," 1999

98 DEGREES
"Give Me Just One Night (Una Noche)," 2000

DESTINY'S CHILD
"Say My Name," 2000

'N SYNC
"Bye Bye Bye," 2000

CHRISTINA AGUILERA
"Genie in a Bottle," 1999;
"Beautiful," 2002

chapter 5

DANCE, DANCE, Dance

R & B-pop sensation Usher is one of the top-selling recording artists of all time. He helped Justin Bieber FACING PAGE in the early days of the teen's career.

BY THE EARLY 2000S, THE VIDEO-SHARING SITE YOUTUBE HAD CHANGED THE WAY AMERICANS LISTENED TO MUSIC.

In the same way that MTV brought music to television, YouTube brought music to computers and smartphones all over the world. Fans could instantly watch their favorite bands and singers online. And new talent could be discovered there too.

For example, thanks to YouTube, a talented teenager named Justin Bieber was discovered. Soon he rocketed to pop superstardom.

THE FEVER

In 2007 Bieber's mom, Patricia Lynn Mallette, set up a YouTube account for her then thirteen-year-old son. She wanted her friends to be able to watch him sing the Ne-Yo song "So Sick" at a talent competition. Bieber's mother continued to upload clips of her son's covers of songs by other R & B artists such as Usher and Stevie Wonder. Like Christina Aguilera and Michael Jackson, Justin Bieber was a little kid with a big voice. He soon had

Listeners sometimes compare Justin Bieber CENTER to Michael Jackson. His vocals can sound like early Michael Jackson, and Bieber has sampled some of Jackson's work in his own material.

fans on YouTube. Seven months after his mother started posting the clips, Bieber flew from his home in Canada to meet with R & B star Usher in the United States.

Usher became Bieber's mentor. By July 2009, Bieber's first single, "One Time," had come out. At that time, Bieber was already No. 23 on YouTube's most-viewed musicians list. The music video for "One Time" was viewed 2 million times in only one month. The first part of his two-part debut album, **My World**,

came out in November 2009. However, before the album was even released, Bieber became one of the only recording artists in music history to have four singles from his first album in the Top 40 of Billboard's Hot 100. **My World 2.0** came out in March 2010. It featured Bieber's biggest hit, the single "Baby."

Like the Jackson 5 and 'N Sync before him, Bieber is a wholesome, clean-cut boy singer. Young female fans find him irresistible. And like other pop stars such as the Beatles

and Madonna, Bieber is famous for his changing hairstyle.

Bieber is also part of a new wave of pop stars who are great at social networking. He keeps in touch with his fans through Facebook and Twitter. In 2010 TV Guide.com reported that—at that time—Bieber accounted for 3 percent of all Twitter traffic.

SOMEONE LIKE YOU

Like Justin Bieber, British singer Adele is another pop star who used social media to help get recognized. Early on, Adele (whose full name is Adele Laurie Blue Adkins) was fascinated by American pop stars such as Pink and Destiny's Child. As a teenager in the United Kingdom, she attended the London School for Performing Arts & Technology (also known as the BRIT School). Her classmates included pop-R & B stylist Leona Lewis. The school's alumni (students from earlier graduating classes) included singer Amy Winehouse.

During Adele's second year at the BRIT school, Shingai Shoniwa, a member of the British indie-rock group the Noisettes, moved in next door to her. The two became friends, and listening to Shoniwa sing made Adele want to sing too.

Surrounded by so much talent and inspiration, Adele decided to try her hand at singing professionally. In 2006 her friend posted a demo tape to the social networking site Myspace. Soon she got an e-mail from a record label executive.

Unlike Justin Bieber, most of whose songs are lighthearted and fun, Adele's songs are usually about pain, heartache, and failed romance. Her debut album, *19* (released in 2008, when she was nineteen years old), was about the down side of love. Her second album, *21* (released in 2011) followed this trend. Songs like "Rolling in the Deep" and "Someone Like You" are sad and deeply emotional. These intense songs help listeners to deal with their own sense of loss or heartache. People can identify with Adele and with the problems that she sings about.

In February 2012, Adele's song "Set Fire to the Rain" became her third No. 1 single in the United States. Adele became the first female pop star in history to lead the Billboard 200 with three simultaneous Billboard Hot 100 No. 1 hits.

Adele got her start as a professional musician after a friend posted one of Adele's homemade recordings on Myspace, where it got the attention of recording executives. She has since become a megastar with fans including Madonna and Beyoncé.

RADIO GAGA

Stefani Joanne Angelina Germanotta grew up in New York City, loving the arts. She learned to play piano and took acting classes as a young girl. She briefly attended New York University and dropped out to pursue a career as a musician. At first, she imagined that she would follow in the footsteps of singer-songwriters such as Fiona Apple and Michelle Branch. But influenced by the work of 1960s painter Andy Warhol and by New York's hip dance-club scene, Germanotta created a theatrical, cartoonish stage personality. She especially loved wearing masks and unusual hats. She called her personality Lady Gaga. She got this name from "Radio Gaga" (1984), a popular song by the rock band Queen.

With her love of crazy costumes, makeup, and provocative lyrics, Lady Gaga is one of the most unique music personalities since the days of glam rock. She has worn everything from an outfit made of raw meat to a dress sewn from tiny Kermit the Frog dolls. And her music is very inspired by glam rock, as well as other types of music.

However, Lady Gaga's work is not all about glam. As with Madonna and Michael Jackson, dance sounds are key to Lady Gaga's appeal. She is a queen of dance-pop. Her songs are hip swinging and very danceable. This is mainly because her work is influenced by disco, which is all about dancing. In fact, Gaga's first single was called "Just Dance" (2008). Her first album, *The Fame* (2008), sold more than one million copies. Critics and fans loved it.

Lady Gaga is an imaginative stage performer who writes her own material. She is an accomplished pianist and always keeps her fans guessing about her next act.

GODS of GLAM ROCK

Glam rock is a type of rock 'n' roll that was very popular in Great Britain during the early 1970s. Glam artists such as David Bowie (LEFT), Gary Glitter, and Freddie Mercury were famous for their theatricality and campiness (finding humor in the ridiculous). They were also known for their outrageous, androgynous (having both male and female traits) makeup and costumes. In fact, Lady Gaga and her makeup remind many people of David Bowie's Ziggy Stardust character. Ziggy was a character Bowie played onstage during the 1970s.

MATERIAL GIRL VERSION 2.0

The similarities between Lady Gaga and Madonna are hard to miss. Both of them were raised Catholic. They both use Catholic symbols in their videos. They both love controversy. They both started out in the New York dance-club scene. And they both support and have a huge following in the gay community.

All the same, Lady Gaga is clearly her own person. Many of her songs—such as her Grammy-winning hit song "Poker Face" (2008)—are about sex, identity, and acceptance. And her song "Born This Way" (2011) sends a clear message: be yourself. Lady Gaga uses her music to address serious issues and to talk about her personal life. Her music is as bold and daring as her costumes.

ONE OF THE GIRLS

Katy Perry likes controversy too. But she doesn't look as if she would. Especially at the beginning of her pop career, she had an old-fashioned 1950s look and her album

> # The best revenge is always success, but the word *revenge* isn't necessarily in my vocabulary.
> —Katy Perry, 2009

cover photos made her seem very wholesome and perky. Her edgy lyrics surprised listeners at first. But they came to expect songs about heartbreak, bad relationships, and wild parties.

Perry was born Katheryn Elizabeth Hudson in Santa Barbara, California, in 1984. She was raised in a very religious household. Her parents are both pastors. As a child, she wasn't allowed to listen to pop music or rock 'n' roll. She started her career recording Christian music. But by the early 2000s, Perry was moving away from her religious upbringing. She changed her name to Katy Perry (her mother's maiden name) so as not to be confused with actress Kate Hudson. And then she started out on a career in pop music.

It took her several years to gain success. But finally in 2008, she launched her first pop album, **One of the Boys**. It landed as No. 9 on the Billboard charts and sold forty-seven thousand copies in its first week.

SCANDALOUS SONGS AND CANDY-COLORED CLOTHES

Two of the songs from **One of the Boys** were controversial. Many listeners felt that "Ur So Gay" was homophobic (hurtful to gay people). However, Perry has said that the song is not meant to mock gay men. Instead, she says it mocks fussy straight men. In addition, some people feel that Perry's song "I Kissed a Girl" was homophobic.

OTHER HIP-POP PIONEERS

Nicki Minaj isn't the only artist to mix pop and hip-hop. Pop stars Fergie (ABOVE), of the Black-Eyed Peas, and Ke$ha sometimes rap on their albums. Also, hip-hop artist Nelly rapped on 'N Sync's 2001 album Celebrity.

These listeners believe that the song uses bisexuality only to sell records. To this, Perry has said that it's a song that many women can relate to. She says she's just being herself and sharing what's on her mind.

Like a lot of female pop stars, Katy Perry is a fashion star. She's known for her vintage (old-fashioned yet stylish) outfits and colorful wigs. Perry often wears candy-colored clothing. In fact, some of her music videos—such as "California Gurls" (2010)—use images of candy and sweets such as lollipops and cupcakes.

THE QUEEN OF HIP-POP

Pop icon Nicki Minaj has much in common with her fellow female pop stars. Like Lady Gaga, Katy Perry, and Ke$ha, Nicki Minaj wears colorful wigs and outrageous glittery makeup in her live stage performances. Like Adele, Minaj owes her career to social media. (She was discovered when Dirty Money Entertainment CEO Fendi listened to her music on her Myspace page.) Like many of her contemporaries, Minaj goes by a stage name. Her real name is Onika Tanya Maraj.

Nicki Minaj performs at a New Year's Eve venue. With a musical style that straddles hip-hop, R & B, and pop, Minaj has risen quickly to the top of the charts. Conquering the male-dominated hip-hop genre, she became the first female artist to be included on MTV's Annual Hottest MCs in the Game List (2011).

She was born in Trinidad in 1984, and Nicki Minaj spent much of her childhood in Queens, New York. In 2009 Minaj signed with Young Money Entertainment, a label run by her musical mentor, Lil Wayne. In November of the following year, she released her first album, **Pink Friday**, which went platinum (sold more than one million copies) within a month after its release. By March 2012, the New York Times was already calling her "the most influential female rapper of all time."

Much like Lady Gaga, who created a cocky male alter ego named Jo Calderone, Nicki Minaj sometimes performs as her cocky male alter ego Roman Zolanski

(named after filmmaker Roman Polanski). In fact, her second album, **Pink Friday: Roman Reloaded** (2012), is built around the Roman Zolanski character.

At first, it seems that Nicki Minaj is very similar to her sisters in pop. Yet unlike Lady Gaga and Ke$ha, whose music is pop with glam rock influences, Nicki Minaj's work is a hybrid of pop and hip-hop. For example, the first half of **Pink Friday: Roman Reloaded** consists of hardcore hip-hop tracks such as "Roman Holiday." The second half consists of bubbly pop tracks such as "Right By My Side." As a Rolling Stone critic said of Minaj's **Roman Reloaded** album, "She doesn't just

straddle pop categories, she dumps them in a Cuisinart, whips them to a frothy purée, then trains a guided missile at the whole mess....But she's a bubblegum starlet as well, delivering confections [treats] to the nation's mall rats."

Until recently, women in rap were not expected to be as outspoken or outrageous as men. However, when Nicki Minaj raps alongside male hip-hop artists such as Jay-Z or Kanye West (both of whom worked with her on the song "Monster," from West's **My Beautiful Dark Twisted Fantasy** album in 2010), she never lets herself take a backseat. She's always on. It's part of why her fans adore her.

POP DIVERSITY

In the 1950s and the early 1960s, pop stars were mostly male and mostly white (pop of that era did have a few female stars, such as Lesley Gore). With the flourishing of bubblegum pop and disco in the late 1960s and 1970s, more female and pop singers of color emerged, such as the Jackson 5 and Donna Summer. In the twenty-first century, the pop scene is very diverse, including many artists of color, such as Nicki Minaj, Bruno Mars, Beyoncé (TOP), Usher, and Rihanna (BOTTOM).

JUST THE WAY POP USED TO BE

Some of the newer pop stars have borrowed from the past to create a retro (old fashioned) look. This is definitely true of Katy Perry, and it's also true of singer-songwriter-producer Bruno Mars. With his pompadour hairstyle and his colorful vintage jackets, he looks as Elvis Presley did in the 1950s. However, even though he looks as if he belongs in the past, his music is very much the music of the present.

Born Peter Gene Hernandez in Honolulu, Hawaii, in 1985, Bruno Mars is one of the biggest pop music acts to come out of Hawaii. He comes from a multicultural showbiz family —his Filipina mother, Bernadette, is a vocalist. His Puerto Rican father, Pete, is a percussionist. Young Bruno (a childhood nickname) used to entertain audiences as a five-year-old Elvis impersonator!

As a young person, Bruno Mars was influenced by musical greats such as Little Richard, Elvis Presley, and Michael Jackson. Like many pop singers, Mars brings a wide range of musical styles, including reggae, R & B, soul, and hip-hop, to his sound.

INTERNATIONAL ICONS of POP

Pop is global. For example, Europe has had many successful pop groups over the years. They include the Swedish group ABBA and the Scottish boy band the Bay City Rollers. The British boy band One Direction (ABOVE) is a huge global phenomenon, and in 2012, they appeared on *Saturday Night Live*. Meanwhile, the Asian pop scene is flourishing. Japanese teen idols include the girl group Morning Musume (LEFT TOP). Rain (Jung Ji-Hoon) is a South Korean pop star. He has been popular worldwide since his debut in 2002. He has even showed up in a few U.S. movies such as *Speed Racer* (2008) and *Ninja Assassin* (2009). Recently, pop singer Charice Pempengco (LEFT BOTTOM), who hails from the Philippines, has appeared on the TV series *Glee* and on Ellen DeGeneres's daytime talk show.

Mars wrote (or cowrote) some of pop music's biggest hits, such as the Travie McCoy's song "Billionaire" (2010) and Cee Lo Green's song "Forget You" (2010). Writing songs for other artists made him want to perform his own material. In July 2010, he got to do just that, when his first single, "Just the Way You Are," was released. It was a gentle, romantic love song with clever lyrics and a catchy melody. The song quickly shot to the top of the Billboard Hot 100.

In October 2010, Mars's first album, **Doo-Wops & Hooligans**, came out. The title of the album was Bruno Mars's way of telling audiences something about himself. He's a big fan of doo-wop music, which is a cappella (voice only) R & B music

from the 1950s. Mars has also explained that the album title means that some of the songs are for women and others are for men. As he told the music blog *Idolator* in 2010, "So doo-wops are for the girls, and hooligans are for the guys." (Hooligan is another name for a gangster or a criminal.)

Although he was influenced by the vocal harmonies and romantic nature of doo-wop music, Bruno Mars's music is twenty-first-century music all the way. For example, his lyrics are usually edgier than what you'd hear in a 1950s song. In "The Lazy Song" (2011), he talks about what he'd do if he just sat around all day and goofed off. The song occasionally talks about sex, definitely a no-no in 1950s pop tunes.

By reaching into the past for inspiration, Bruno Mars has created an interesting new type of twenty-first-century pop.

THE FUTURE OF POP

What does the future hold for pop music? It's always hard to tell. For example, no one could have predicted Madonna's long-lasting fame. But catchy melodies are always key. So are danceable songs and exciting hooks. One thing is for sure: New musical styles will always influence pop music. And young people will always love pop songs. Long live pop! ★

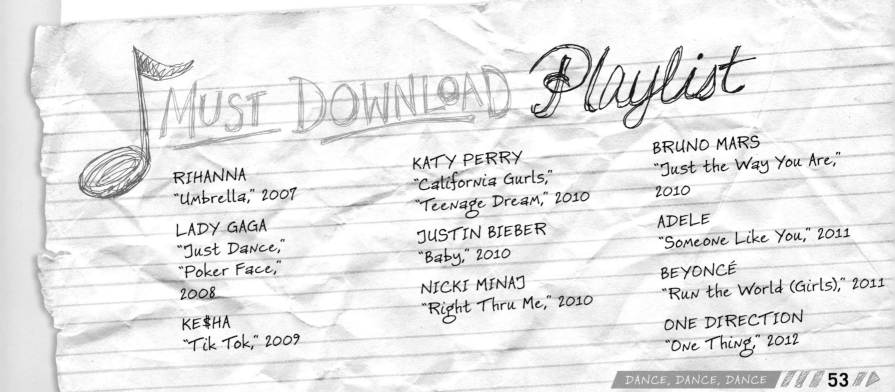

♫ MUST DOWNLOAD Playlist

RIHANNA
"Umbrella," 2007

LADY GAGA
"Just Dance,"
"Poker Face,"
2008

KE$HA
"Tik Tok," 2009

KATY PERRY
"California Gurls,"
"Teenage Dream," 2010

JUSTIN BIEBER
"Baby," 2010

NICKI MINAJ
"Right Thru Me," 2010

BRUNO MARS
"Just the Way You Are,"
2010

ADELE
"Someone Like You," 2011

BEYONCÉ
"Run the World (Girls)," 2011

ONE DIRECTION
"One Thing," 2012

GLOSSARY

bass: a sound that is in the lowest musical pitch or range

bubblegum pop: a type of pop music that is aimed at children and tweens

dance-pop: a type of pop music that focuses on loud, pulsating beats and danceable melodies. Dance-pop music developed after disco.

disc jockey: a person who introduces and plays recorded pop music, especially in a club or on the radio; also called a DJ

disco: a popular dance music style of the 1970s. Disco has electronic sounds, catchy rhythms, and repetitive lyrics.

discotheque: a nightclub where people dance to recorded pop music; also called disco

harmony: a combination of tones that is played or sung at the same time and that is pleasing to the ear

MTV: a television network that launched on August 1, 1981. MTV plays music videos, reality shows, original scripted series, and other music- and pop culture-based programming.

music video: a short film or video that accompanies a song or piece of music

pop: a genre of music that is appealing to a large audience of kids, teens, and young adults. The modern form of pop music originated in the 1950s and was based on rock 'n' roll. However, more recent pop music has other influences, including funk, hip-hop, and disco.

R & B: rhythm and blues music. This music came out of the African American communities of the American South. The term *R & B* usually refers to soul and funk music.

rock 'n' roll: a type of pop music that evolved from a combination of blues, jazz, country, and gospel music

race records: gospel, jazz, or R & B albums for and by African Americans. Race records were very popular during the 1940s and the 1950s. White Americans discovered them in the 1950s and began to copy the sound of the music and the dance moves associated with them.

video jockey: someone who announces, plays, and comments on music videos. Video jockeys (VJs) are frequently seen on TV networks such as MTV and VH1.

TIMELINE

1949: Fats Domino records "The Fat Man," considered by some to be the first rock 'n' roll record.

1954: At Sun Studios in Memphis, Tennessee, Elvis Presley records the song "That's All Right, Mama," marking his debut as a rock 'n' roll performer.

1957: Paul Anka performs his first hit pop song, "Diana," on the *Ed Sullivan Show*.

1959: Bobby Darin records a bouncy, pop-infused cover of the 1928 song "Mack the Knife."

1964: The Beatles perform on the *Ed Sullivan Show* for the first time. Beatlemania is born.

1968: Pioneering bubblegum pop group 1910 Fruitgum Company releases its first single, "Simon Says."

1969: The Jackson 5, the first African American bubblegum pop group, releases their first No. 1 hit single, "I Want You Back."

1970: The TV series *The Partridge Family*, about a fictional pop group, launches. It is on the air until 1974.

1971: The Osmonds release their hit record, *One Bad Apple*.

1973: The first article on disco music appears in *Rolling Stone* magazine.

1977: The film *Saturday Night Fever*, about a working-class kid who loves disco music, is released and becomes a huge hit. The movie's sound track, full of Bee Gees songs, is a big success.

1981: MTV makes its debut. The first music video to be aired on the television network is the Buggles' "Video Killed the Radio Star."

1983: New Edition releases its first album, *Candy Girl*. The album signals the return of bubblegum pop.

1984: Madonna's second album, *Like a Virgin*, is released. It is her first album to reach No. 1 on the U.S. charts.

1988: The New Kids on the Block's second album, *Hangin' Tough*, is released. The album stays on the *Billboard 200* for 113 weeks, eventually reaching the No. 1 spot.

1995: The Backstreet Boys' self-titled debut album is a huge hit overseas.

1998: Britney Spears releases her debut album, *One More Time*.

2007: Justin Bieber's mother posts a YouTube video of her son performing "So Sick" at a local talent competition.

2008: Lady Gaga releases her debut album, *The Fame*.

2011: Adele releases her second album, *21*, which features such hit songs as "Someone Like You."

2012: The British boy band One Direction is featured on *Saturday Night Live*.

MINI BIOS

The Bee Gees: The Bee Gees were an Australian musical group of three brothers, Barry (b. 1946), Robin (1949–2012), and Maurice Gibb (1949–2003). They started out in the 1960s as a pop group. In the mid-1970s, they became disco superstars. In 1977 they provided several songs for the sound track of the hit film *Saturday Night Fever*.

Bobby Darin (1936–1973): Born in the Bronx, New York, Darin was an accomplished singer and musician. He could play many different instruments. Darin became famous during the 1950s and the 1960s with pop songs such as "Splish Splash" (1958) and "Mack the Knife" (1959). In 1973, after heart surgery, Darin died at the age of thirty-seven.

Michael Jackson (1958–2009): Starting at the age of eleven, Michael Jackson was a singer in the boy band the Jackson 5 with his four older brothers. In the 1970s, Michael began a successful solo career. In the 1980s, he starred in groundbreaking music videos for many of his songs, including "Billie Jean" (1983), "Beat It" (1983), and "Thriller" (1984). After an amazing career, during which he sold an estimated 750 million records worldwide, Michael Jackson died of a drug overdose in 2009.

Jerry Kasenetz and Jeff Katz (born 1943): These two pop music producers from Brooklyn, New York, coined the term *bubblegum pop*. Working throughout the late 1960s, Kasenetz and Katz were known as Super K Productions. Super K produced albums by such bubblegum pop groups as 1910 Fruitgum Company and the Ohio Express.

Lady Gaga (born 1986): New York City pop star Lady Gaga (born Stefani Joanne Angelina Germanotta) began her career wanting to be a serious singer-songwriter. After being part of New York's dance club scene, she chose a stage personality she called Lady Gaga. Gaga is as well known for her over-the-top fashion sense as she is for her clever lyrics and pounding beats. Her hit songs include "Poker Face" (2008) and "Born This Way" (2011).

Bruno Mars (born 1985): A pop star and songwriter from Honolulu, Hawaii, Bruno Mars (born Peter Gene Hernandez) comes from a showbiz family. Mars is known for his soul pop vocal style, sometimes compared to that of Michael Jackson, and for his clever lyrics. His hit songs include "Just the Way You Are" (2010) and "Grenade" (2010).

'N Sync: The members of this boy band were Justin Timberlake (b. 1981), J. C. Chasez (b. 1976), Chris Kirkpatrick (b. 1971), Joey Fatone (b. 1977), and Lance Bass (b. 1979). After performing in Europe, 'N Sync released a self-titled debut album in the United States in 1998. Soon, 'N Sync shot to superstardom. In 2007 the band announced they had officially broken up.

Elvis Presley (1935–1977): A very talented performer from Mississippi, Presley was influenced by the blues, country music, and gospel. Presley almost by himself brought rock music to mainstream America during the 1950s. He died following a heart attack at Graceland, his home in Memphis, Tennessee.

Britney Spears (born 1981): A pop star and dancer from McComb, Mississippi, Spears started out on the All-New *Mickey Mouse Club* TV show. She is one of a handful of teen idols who helped bring back bubblegum pop in the late 1990s. Her hit songs include "... Baby One More Time" (1998), "Toxic" (2004), and "Womanizer" (2008).

POP MUST-HAVES

Fats Domino, "The Fat Man" (1949)

Kings of Rhythm, "Rocket '88'" (1951)

Muddy Waters, "Hoochie Coochie Man" (1954)

Elvis Presley, "That's All Right" (1954)

Paul Anka, "Diana" (1957)

Bobby Darin, "Mack the Knife" (1959)

Lesley Gore, "It's My Party" (1963)

Beatles, "I Want to Hold Your Hand" (1963)

Monkees, "Daydream Believer" (1967)

1910 Fruitgum Company, "Simon Says" (1968)

Archies, "Sugar, Sugar" (1969)

Jackson 5, "ABC" (1970)

Osmonds, "One Bad Apple" (1970)

Partridge Family, "I Think I Love You" (1970)

Hues Corporation, "Rock the Boat" (1974)

KC and the Sunshine Band, "Get Down Tonight" (1975)

Bee Gees, "Stayin' Alive" (1977)

Gloria Gaynor, "I Will Survive" (1978)

Buggles, "Video Killed the Radio Star" (1979)

Michael Jackson, "Thriller" (1982)

Madonna, "Material Girl" (1985)

New Edition, "Candy Girl" (1983)

New Kids on the Block, "I'll Be Loving You (Forever)" (1989)

Tiffany, "I Think We're Alone Now" (1987)

Debbie Gibson, "Lost in Your Eyes" (1989)

Spice Girls, "Wannabe" (1996)

Backstreet Boys, "Quit Playing Games (With My Heart)" (1997)

Britney Spears, "...Baby One More Time" (1998)

'N Sync, "Bye Bye Bye" (2000)

Christina Aguilera, "Beautiful" (2002)

Lady Gaga, "Just Dance," "Poker Face" (2008)

Justin Bieber, "Baby" (2010)

Katy Perry, "California Gurls," "Teenage Dream" (2010)

Adele, "Someone Like You" (2011)

Bruno Mars, "The Lazy Song" (2011)

One Direction, "One Thing" (2012)

MAJOR AWARDS

American Music Awards (AMAs): The AMA ceremony is broadcast each year on the ABC television network. TV host Dick Clark created the AMAs in 1973. Unlike the Grammy Awards, the AMAs are awarded based on polls of the public. Eminem took home the 2010 awards for Favorite Male Artist and Favorite Album in the Rap/Hip-Hop category. In 2011 Adele won for Favorite Female Artist and Favorite Album (*21*).

Grammy Awards: The Grammys are prestigious music awards given yearly since 1959 by the National Academy of Recording Arts and Sciences. Adele carried home Grammy Awards in pop categories in 2012 for Best Pop Solo Performance, "Someone Like You," and for Best Pop Vocal Album (*21*).

MTV Video Music Awards (VMAs): The VMAs were started in 1984. MTV VMA 2011 winners for pop categories included Justin Bieber for Best Male Video, "U Smile"; Lady Gaga for Best Female Video, "Born This Way"; and Britney Spears for Best Pop Video, "Till the World Ends."

SOURCE NOTES

8   Jann Wenner, ed. "Rolling Stone: The *100 Greatest Artists of All Time*," special issue, 2011, 21.

8   Ibid., 12.

17   Kim Cooper, and David Smay, eds., *Bubblegum Music Is the Naked Truth* (Los Angeles: Feral House, 2001), 185.

22   Neil McCormick, "Bee Gees Interview." *Telegraph* (London), November 4, 2009, http://www.telegraph .co.uk/culture/music/rockandpopfeatures/6502249/Bee-Gees-interview .html (September 23, 2011).

23   Bernard Weinraub, "Here's to Disco, It Never Could Say Goodbye." *New York Times*, December 10, 2002, http:// www.nytimes.com/2002/12/10/arts /arts-in-america-here-s-to-disco-it-never-could-say-goodbye.html (October 18, 2011)

28   Jocelyn Vena, "Justin Timberlake on Michael Jackson: He 'Was the Baddest!'" MTV.com, http://www.mtv. com/news/articles/1615005/justin-timberlake-on-michael-jackson-was-baddest.jhtml (June 17, 2011).

39   Jane Stevenson, "Spears Takes Aim at Fame," Jam! Showbiz—Music, July 10, 1999, http://jam.canoe .ca/Music/Artists/S/Spears_ Britney/1999/07/10/749831.html (September 23, 2011).

47   Johnson Publishing, "Katy Perry—Hot N Bold," *Scotsman.com*, February 17, 2009, http://www.scotsman.com/ news/interview_katy_perry_hot_n_ bold_1_829754 (September 23, 2011).

50   Jon Caramanica, "A Singular Influence," *New York Times*, March 30, 2012. http://www.nytimes .com/2012/04/01 /arts/music/nicki-minaj-is-the-influential-leader-of-hip-hop.html?_ r=2&adxnnl=1&seid=auto &smid=tw-nytimesmusic &adxnnlx=1336968402-ISA6K-aGZq5kOHn/YeG2vvA (April 23, 2012).

50 Jody Rosen. "Nicki Minaj, Pink Friday: Roman Reloaded Review," Rolling Stone, April 6, 2012, http://www .rollingstone.com/music /albumreviews/pink-friday-roman-reloaded-20120406#ixzz1rlivwsyl (April 23, 2012).

53 Cynthia DeCastro. "Bruno Mars: The Fil-Am Artist with Universal Appeal." Asian Journal. January 5, 2011. http:// www.asianjournal.com/aj-magazine /midweek-mgzn/8386-bruno-mars-the-fil-am-artist-withuniversal-appeal.html (June 11, 2012).

SELECTED BIBLIOGRAPHY

Ali, Lorraine. "The Anti-Gaga." Newsweek, October 7, 2010. http://www .thedailybeast.com /newsweek/2010/10/07/kesha-setting-sales-records.html (March 23, 2012).

Baltin, Steve. "Who Is Max Martin? A Hit-Making 'Beast.'" Popeater, October 14, 2009. http://www.popeater .com/2009/10/14/who-is max-martin/ (September 23, 2011).

BBC. "The Bee Gees: Brothers in Harmony." BBC News.com. December 31, 2001. http://news.bbc.co.uk/2/hi /entertainment/1734797.stm (August 2, 2011).

BBC. "'New' Jackson Song Penned in 1983." BBC News.com. October 13, 2009. Accessed June 17, 2011. http://news.bbc.co.uk/2/hi/entertainment/8304118.stm

Caramanica, Jon. "A Singular Influence," New York Times, March 30, 2012. http://www.nytimes.com/2012/04/01 /arts/music/nicki-minaj-is-the-influential-leader-of-hip-hop.html?_r=2&adxnnl=1&seid=auto&smid=tw-nytimesmusic&adxnnlx=1336968402-ISA6KaGZq5kOHn /YeG2vvA (April 23, 2012).

Chu, Jeff. "Top of the Pops." Time Magazine, March 19, 2001. http://www.time. com/time/magazine /article/0,9171,102126,00.html (June 17, 2011).

Cooper, Kim, and David Smay, eds. Bubble-gum Music Is the Naked Truth. Los Angeles: Feral House, 2001.

CNN. "MTV Won't Say How Old It Is (But It's 25): A List of Music Television's Notable Moments." CNN.com. August 1, 2006. http://web.archive .org/web/20060811230032/http:// www.cnn.com/2006/SHOWBIZ /Music/08/01/mtv.at.25.ap/index .html (June 17, 2011).

DeCastro, Cynthia. "Bruno Mars: The Fil-Am Artist with Universal Appeal." Asian Journal. January 5, 2011. http://www.asianjournal.com/ aj-magazine/midweek-mgzn/8386-bruno-mars-the-fil-am-artist-with-universal-appeal.html (March 23, 2012).

Dundy, Elaine. Elvis and Gladys. New York: Macmillan Publishing Company, 1985.

Entertainment Weekly. "The 100 Greatest Moments in Rock Music: The '80s." EW.com. May 28, 1999. http://www .ew.com/ew/article/0,,273505,00 .html (June 17, 2011).

Essex, Andrew, and Dave Karger. "Bubble Gum Blows Up!" Entertainment Weekly. March 5, 1999. http://www.ew.com /ew/article/0,,274628,00.html (September 23, 2011).

Gore, Chris. The 50 Greatest Movies Never Made. New York: St. Martin's Griffin, 1999.

Hogan, Ed. "The Partridge Family: Biography." Allmusic. N.d. http://www .allmusic.com/artist/the-partridge-family-p5111/biography (September 23, 2011).

Kellogg, Valerie. "Q&A with Music Icon Paul Anka." Popmatters.com. November 14, 2008. http://www.popmatters .com/pm/article/65731-qa-with-music-icon-paul-anka (September 23, 2011).

Killmeier, Matthew A. "Race Music." St. James Encyclopedia of Pop Culture. January 29, 2002. http://findarticles .com/p/articles/mi_g1epc/is_tov/ ai_2419101005/pg_2/?tag=mantle_ skin;content (September 23, 2011).

Lamb, Bill. "Top 10 Teen Pop Artists of All Time." About.com. N.d. http://top40 .about.com/od/top10lists/tp/teenpo-partists.htm (August 2, 2011).

Lennon, John. John Lennon: In His Own Write & A Spaniard in the Works. New York: Signet, 1967.

McCormick, Neil. "Bee Gees Interview." Telegraph (London), November 4, 2009. http://www.telegraph.co.uk /culture/music/rockandpopfea-tures/6502249/Bee-Gees-interview .html (September 23, 2011).

NPR. "The 50 Most Important Recordings of the Decade." All Songs Considered. NPR Music. November 16, 2009. http://www.npr. org/2009/11/16/120400577/the-50-most-important-recordings-s-z (September 23, 2011).

O'Hagan, Sean. "Fifty Years of Pop." The Observer, May 1, 2004. Accessed June 17, 2011. http://www.guardian.co.uk/ music/2004/may/02/popandrock/print

Oseary, Guy. Jews Who Rock. New York: St. Martin's Press, 2001.

Pareles, Jon. "Barry White, Disco-Era Crooner, Dies at 58." New York Times, July 4, 2003. http://www.nytimes. com/2003/07/04 /obituaries/04WIRE-WHITE-OBIT .html (August 2, 2011).

Prato, Greg. MTV Ruled the World: The Early Years of Music Video. Raleigh: Lulu.com, 2010.

Raymond, Usher. "Justin Bieber: The Crown Prince of Pop." Time Magazine, May 2, 2011, 88.

Rosen, Jody. "Nicki Minaj, Pink Friday: Roman Reloaded Review." Rolling Stone, April 6, 2012. http://www .rollingstone.com/music/albumre-views/pink-friday-roman-reloaded-20120406#ixzz1rlivwsyl (April 23, 2012).

Roylance, Brian, Julian Quance, Oliver Craske, and Roman Milisic, Eds. The Beatles Anthology. San Francisco: Chronicle Books, 2000.

Schoemer, Karen. "Ringo and a band of Starrs." New York Times, June 22, 1992. http://www.nytimes.com/1992/06/22 /arts/reviews-music-ringo-and-a-band-of-stars.html (August 2, 2011).

Scotsman.com, "Katy Perry—Hot N Bold." February 17, 2009. http:// www.scotsman.com/news/interview_ katy_perry_hot_n_bold_1_829754 (September 23, 2011).

Stevenson, Jane. "Paul Anka Will Always Do It His Way." Jam! Showbiz—Music. February 29, 2008. http://jam .canoe.ca/Music/Artists/A/Anka_ Paul/2008/02/29/4883738-sun.html (September 23, 2011).

———. "Spears Takes Aim at Fame." Jam! Showbiz—Music. July 10, 1999. http://jam.canoe.ca/Music /Artists/S/Spears_Brit-ney/1999/07/10/749831.html (September 23, 2011).

Sunday Star-Times (Fairfax, NZ). "Katy Perry: Girl Trouble." October 24, 2008. http://www.stuff.co.nz/sunday-star-times/entertainment/more-entertainment-stories/688815 (September 23, 2011).

Swartz, Shauna. "Interview with Lesley Gore." AfterEllen.com. June 3, 2005. http://www.afterellen.com/People/2005/6/lesleygore.html (August 2, 2011).

Thompson, Gordon. Please Please Me: Sixties British Pop, Inside Out. New York: Oxford University Press, 2008.

Vena, Jocelyn. "Justin Timberlake on Michael Jackson: He 'Was the Baddest!'" MTV.com. June 30, 2009. http://www.mtv.com/news/articles/1615005/justin-timberlake-on-michael-jackson-was-baddest.jhtml (June 17, 2011).

Vigilante, David. "Commentary: Jackson Was the Jackie Robinson of MTV." CNN.com, June 26, 2009. . http://articles.cnn.com/2009-06-26/entertainment/vigilante.jackson_1_mtv-raps-music-video-rock-song?_s=PM:SHOWBIZ (June 17, 2011).

Weinraub, Bernard. "Here's to Disco, It Never Could Say Goodbye." New York Times, December 10, 2002. http://www.nytimes.com/2002/12/10/arts/arts-in-america-here-s-to-disco-it-never-could-say-goodbye.html (October 18, 2011).

FURTHER READING, WEBSITES, AND FILMS

Allmusic.
http://www.allmusic.com
Beginning in 1992, All Music Guide (AMG) has published a series of reference books on music. Since 1995 the allmusic website has been a place for music fans to look up their favorite performers, research out-of-print recordings, or read reviews of new releases. The knowledgeable AMG editorial staff makes sure that this site covers all genres and styles of music.

Austerlitz, Saul. Money for Nothing: A History of the Music Video from the Beatles to the White Stripes. New York: Continuum, 2008.
Find out more about the history of the music video, including its origins, conventions, stars, and clichés.

Bass, Lance, and Marc Eliot. Out of Sync: A Memoir. New York: Simon Spotlight Entertainment, 2007.
In this book, former 'N Sync member Lance Bass talks about his life as a pop star, the difficulties of celebrity, and what led him to come out of the closet as an openly gay man at the age of twenty-seven.

Behnke, Alison Marie. Death of a Dreamer: The Assassination of John Lennon. Minneapolis: Twenty-First Century Books, 2012.
In this well-researched title, Behnke explores the lives of John Lennon and his assassin Mark David Chapman. She follows the two men as they head toward the tragic day in 1980 when Chapman shot and killed the pop superstar in New York City. Learn more about what may have motivated Chapman and about Lennon's legacy.

Beyond the Sea. DVD. Directed by Kevin Spacey. Produced by Jan Fantl, Arthur E. Friedman, and Andy Paterson. Santa Monica, CA: Lions Gate Films, 2004.
This film is a musical biography that explores the life and career of 1950s pop star Bobby Darin. It stars Kevin Spacey as Bobby Darrin, and Kate Bosworth as Sandra Dee, the popular movie star who marries Bobby.

Doeden, Matt. *Lady Gaga: Pop's Glam Queen*. Minneapolis: Twenty-First Century Books, 2012.
This is a fun overview of Lady Gaga's life and career. Learn about her beginnings in art school in New York City, her musical influences, and her rise to superstardom.

Guralnick, Peter, and Ernst Jorgensen. *Elvis Day by Day, The Definitive Record of His Life and Music*. New York: Ballantine Books, 1999.
A fascinating day-by-day, year-by-year chronicle of Elvis Presley's life and career. This book was a collaboration between two well-known Presley biographers, who were given unusual access to Graceland and the Elvis Presley Enterprises archives there.

Jackson, Michael. *Moonwalk*. New York: Crown, 2009.
In pop music legend Michael Jackson's autobiography, he writes about his life, his career, and his relationships. The book includes a foreword from the original edition by former first lady Jacqueline Kennedy Onassis and a new introduction by Motown founder Berry Gordy.

Krohn, Kate. *Michael Jackson: Ultimate Music Legend*. Minneapolis: Lerner Publications, 2010.
Read about Michael Jackson's musical career and what made him the pop legend he became.

Marks, Craig, and Rob Tannenbaum. *I Want My MTV: The Uncensored Story of the Music Video Revolution*. New York: Dutton Adult, 2011.
This book gives a detailed history of the first decade of MTV's existence. Learn more about how MTV changed music, television, fashion, and even politics.

Osmond, Donny, and Patricia Romanowski. *Life Is Just What You Make It: My Story So Far*. New York : Hyperion, 2006.
Find out more about Donny Osmond's life as a pop star through this revealing memoir.

Roberts, Jeremy. *The Beatles: Music Revolutionaries*. Minneapolis: Twenty-First Century Books, 2011.
This book gives a good overview of the Beatles and their music. Learn how the band came together in Liverpool, England, in the 1960s and shot to stardom in the United States.

Spears, Britney, and Lynn Spears. *Britney Spears' Heart to Heart*. New York: Three Rivers Press, 2000.
This book is written by Britney Spears and her mother. It is an inspirational story about Spears's journey from talent shows in Kentwood, Louisiana, to pop superstardom. The book also explores mother-daughter relationships and how parents and children can work together to overcome obstacles.

Temporal, Paul. *The Branding of MTV: Will Internet Kill the Video Star*. Indianapolis: Wiley Publishing, 2008.
Find out more about how MTV made itself known to the public, how it became a global phenomenon, and how it continues to market itself in the digital age.

INDEX

ABOUT THE AUTHOR

Arie Kaplan began his career writing about pop music for magazines such as Teen Beat, Tiger Beat, and BOP. Over the years, he has also satirized pop music as a writer for Mad Magazine. He's the author of the acclaimed nonfiction book From Krakow to Krypton: Jews and Comic Books, a 2008 finalist for the National Jewish Book Award.

As a nonfiction author, Kaplan has written numerous books for young readers on subjects ranging from the life of Vlad the Impaler to teens and relationships. Kaplan has also written comics and graphic novels for DC Comics, Archie Comics, Bongo Comics, IDW, and other companies. Please check out his website, www.ariekaplan.com.

PHOTO ACKNOWLEDGMENTS

The images in this book are used with the permission of: © John A. Angelillo/CORBIS, p. 1; © Sandy Young/Alamy, p. 2; © Steve Granitz/WireImage/Getty Images, p. 3; © Paramount Pictures/Moviepix/Getty Images, p. 4; © Gilles Petard/Redferns/Getty Images, p. 5; © Tony Evans/Timelapse Library Ltd./Hulton Archive/Getty Images, p. 6; © Martha Holmes/Time & Life/Getty Images, p. 7; © Frank Driggs Collection/Archive Photos/Getty Images, p. 8; © AF Archive/Alamy, p. 9; © CBS Photo Archive/Getty Images, p. 10 (top); © Hulton Archive/Getty Images, pp. 10 (bottom), 21 (top right); © David Redfern/Redferns/Getty Images, pp. 11, 17; © Jeff Kravitz/FilmMagic/Getty Images, p. 12; AP Photo, p. 13 (left); © iStockphoto.com/hudiemm, pp. 13 (right), 23, 35 (bottom), 41 (right), 53, 55, 57, 59, 61, 63; © Michael Ochs Archives/Getty Images, pp. 14, 15, 16, 20 (bottom), 21 (bottom), 22, 25 (top), 34; © Anwar Hussein/Hulton Archive/Getty Images, p. 18; © GAB Archive/Redferns/Getty Images, pp. 19, 27 (left); © Tim Hall/Redferns/Getty Images, p. 20 (top); © Michael Putland/Hulton Archive/Getty Images, p. 21 (top left); © Neal Preston/CORBIS, pp. 24, 30, 33, 36; Courtesy Everett Collection, p. 25 (bottom); © Gered Mankowitz/Redferns/Getty Images, p. 26; © Fin Costello/Redferns/Getty Images, p. 27 (right); © MCA/Universal/Courtesy Everett Collection, p. 29; © David McGough/DMI/Time & Life Pictures/Getty Images, p. 31; Eugene Adebari/Rex USA, p. 32; © Paul Natkin/WireImage/Getty Images, p. 35 (top); © Mark Weiss/WireImage/Getty Images, p. 37; Everett Collection/Rex USA, p. 38; © Timothy A. Clary/AFP/Getty Images, p. 39; © Ethan Miller/CORBIS, p. 40; © Tim Roney/Hulton Archive/Getty Images, p. 41 (left); © Dimitrios Kambouris/WireImage/Getty Images, p. 42; © Mark Ashman/Disney Parks/Getty Images, p. 43; © John Shearer/WireImage/Getty Images, pp. 44, 51; Imaginechina via AP Images, p. 45; © Chris Walter/WireImage/Getty Images, p. 46; © Neil Lupin/Getty Images, p. 47; AP Photo/PRNewsFoto/wet n wild, p. 48; © Kevin Winter/DCNYRE2012/Getty Images, p. 49; © Mike Coppola/Getty Images, p. 50 (top); © Robyn Beck/AFP/Getty Images, p. 50 (bottom); © Fred Duval/FilmMagic/Getty Images, p. 52 (top); © Han Myung-Gu/WireImage/Getty Images, p. 52 (middle); © Paul Archuleta/FilmMagic/Getty Images, p. 52 (bottom).

Front cover: © Banauke/Shutterstock.com (disco ball); © iStockphoto.com/Johnnyhetfield (singer).
Back cover: © iStockphoto.com/hudiemm.

Main body text set in Arta Std Book 12/14
Typeface provided by International Typeface Corp